W9-ACE-913

SEQUOYA

Library of Congress Number: 87-32319

Library of Congress Cataloging in Publication Data

Gleiter, Jan, 1947-
    Sequoya.

    (Raintree stories)
    Summary: A biography of the Cherokee Indian who
invented a system of writing for his people in the
early nineteenth century and after whom the giant
sequoia trees and Sequoia National Park were named.
    1. Sequoya, 1770?—1843.   2. Cherokee Indians—
Biography—Juvenile literature.   3. Indians of North
America—Biography——Juvenile literature.   4. Cherokee
Indians—Writing—Juvenile literature.   5. Indians of
North America—Writing—Juvenile literature.
[1. Sequoya, 1770?-1843.   2. Cherokee Indians—
Biography.   3. Indians of North America—Biography]
I. Thompson, Kathleen.   II. Title.
E99.C5S384   1988   970.004'97   [B]   [92]   87-32319
ISBN 0-8172-2678-8 (lib. bdg.)
ISBN 0-8172-2682-6 (softcover)

SEQUOYA

Jan Gleiter and Kathleen Thompson

Illustrated by Tom Redman

Raintree Childrens Books
Milwaukee

It was early spring in the year 1814. A weary man was on his way home to Tennessee from the War of 1812. His name was Sequoya, but he was often called "The Lame One" because of an injured leg that caused him to limp. He was a Cherokee Indian. He had fought on the American side in this war, fought along with white soldiers and other Cherokee against the British and the Creek Indians. Now, with the war nearly over, he had been released from the army.

When Sequoya reached his cabin, he jumped
from his pony. His daughter, Ah-yoka, came
running. He swung her into the air and laughed
with the happiness of being home.

He looked around at the cornfields and the rest
of the small farm. His family had worked hard
while he was gone. The corn was already planted
for this year's crop. Sequoya was glad. There was
something he wanted to do—something that had
nothing to do with farming, trading furs, making
things from silver, or any of the other things at
which he was skilled.

An idea had been burning in his mind for years. He wanted to find a way to write the Cherokee language. And he would need all his time and all his energy to do it.

Some of the Cherokee Indians had gone to English-speaking schools and had learned to speak, read, and write that language. But they could not read or write their own language; they could only speak it. The reason was that there *was* no written Cherokee language. There was no way to write down a story or something that had been learned. The Cherokee had to remember everything they had been told—remember and pass their memories along to their children.

Sequoya couldn't help but think that if the Cherokee could write their language, it would be like catching and taming a wild pony. Their language could be caught and held and made to serve them. Their knowledge would not be lost.

In the army, Sequoya had seen white soldiers get letters from home. While he wondered and worried about his family, he saw other soldiers tear open papers and laugh with joy as they looked at the marks on them. He himself did not know English, and he wondered at how these people could send their words on paper over long distances. Sequoya called the papers "talking leaves." They were an amazing thing.

Some of his friends thought that writing was a gift that God had given to white people. It had not been given to the Cherokee, so they would have to make do without it. Sequoya disagreed. He thought that white people had made this gift of writing themselves. And if they could, he could.

Sequoya did not realize that no one person had
ever made a written language before. He had
no way to know that other written languages had
been developed over hundreds and thousands of
years. He didn't understand what many other
people did understand—that it was an almost
impossible job for one person. While his sons took
care of the farm, Sequoya sat with Ah-yoka and
drew pictures. He had decided to draw a simple
picture for each word in the Cherokee language.
He scratched his pictures with the tip of a knife, or
he drew them with a piece of coal or a burnt stick.

L ook," he would say. "What is this?"
    Ah-yoka, who loved to play this game, would
peer at the tiny drawing. "It's a horse!" she would
say, or a bear, or an arrow, or a knife, or whatever
it was that her father had drawn.

"Yes," Sequoya would answer. "That is the picture for horse." And he would set it aside on the pile of bark that grew higher every day.

Sequoya's friends worried about him. They tried to persuade him that his dream was hopeless and foolish. There were many things that needed doing, and he wasn't doing them. He should be working his farm. It was becoming overgrown with weeds. He should be trading furs, making salt, and building the things he built so well. Instead, he was wasting his time making pictures on bark.

Sequoya tried to explain how important his idea was and how useful it would be to have a way to write the Cherokee words. It would help all their people for all time. Couldn't they see that? But they shook their heads and walked away. Pretty soon, Sequoya stopped trying to explain. He just listened politely to the criticism and kept right on doing what he was doing.

And then one day, all of his pictures were
destroyed in a fire. Months and months of
work, of thinking about all the words he knew, of
finding ways to draw them—had gone up in smoke.
He began again. He started to use a brush he had
made from animal hair, and paints that he made
from plants.

When the new pile of bark pictures was very high, Sequoya realized that there were words he could not draw. He could not draw a word for *go*. It would look just like the word for *walk*. He could draw the word for *bird*. But how could he draw all the different birds, so that anyone looking at the simple pictures could tell which bird he meant?

Sequoya thought about the English words he had seen. They were very different from the pictures he had drawn. They used the same shapes over and over again. But the way they were put together was different. It was a puzzle. How were those words made? How did anyone know what they meant?

Suddenly it came to him. The shapes had to do with sounds, not with meaning. If he used a shape to stand for the sound *ah*, that shape could be used at the end of his name and at the beginning of his daughter Ah-yoka's. The same shape could be used in every Cherokee word that had the sound *ah* in it. Yes! That was it! All his energy came sweeping back. He pushed aside the drawings and began one more time.

Ah-yoka was a great help to him. His own ears were not as good as hers. She could hear differences in word sounds and make him hear them too, by saying them slowly, over and over. And her memory was helpful. Together they thought of every word they knew. Sequoya listened to everyone he could find. He was on a hunt, a hunt for words and sounds.

In 1818, Sequoya and his family moved to the territory of Arkansas. White settlers in Tennessee wanted the Cherokee land, and many of the Cherokee took the offer of new land farther west. Sequoya took his dream with him, together with the brushes and paints he was using to make his dream come true.

Whenever he thought of a syllable from the Cherokee language, he made a symbol or shape for it. Then he combined the ones that had very similar sounds. Finally, he came up with eighty-six symbols. Many looked like English letters, but they were sideways or upside down. Some looked like Greek letters. Some he made up. Each one stood for a syllable. So, by learning only eighty-six shapes, a person could read any word in the Cherokee language.

By 1821, Sequoya's written language was finished. The only problem he faced now was convincing the tribe's leaders that it worked. It was time to share the dream. He took Ah-yoka and traveled back east to meet with tribal leaders.

These leaders were willing to meet with Sequoya. But they were not at all sure that he wasn't crazy. Many people thought he had been practicing witchcraft all those years with his pictures and shapes. They had to be shown that he had made a way to put words into writing.

So Sequoya told his daughter to stay in a room with the leaders. He told her to write down what they told her. Then he came back into the room and read what she had written. The leaders had to admit that what he said was true. Words could be written down. Finally they agreed to let him try to teach some of their young men to read and write the language. The young men learned very quickly.

Before long, news of the written language had spread everywhere. Cherokee men, women, and children came eagerly to be taught. Soon there were Cherokee words painted on trees, carved into posts, and drawn on walls and fences. Within a few months, thousands of Cherokee had learned to read and write their language. The Cherokee who lived in Arkansas wrote to their relatives and friends who still lived in Tennessee. The eastern Cherokee wrote back. A newspaper was begun, the *Cherokee Phoenix*. Cherokee stories, songs, and prayers were written down. Schoolbooks and Bibles were printed in the Cherokee language.

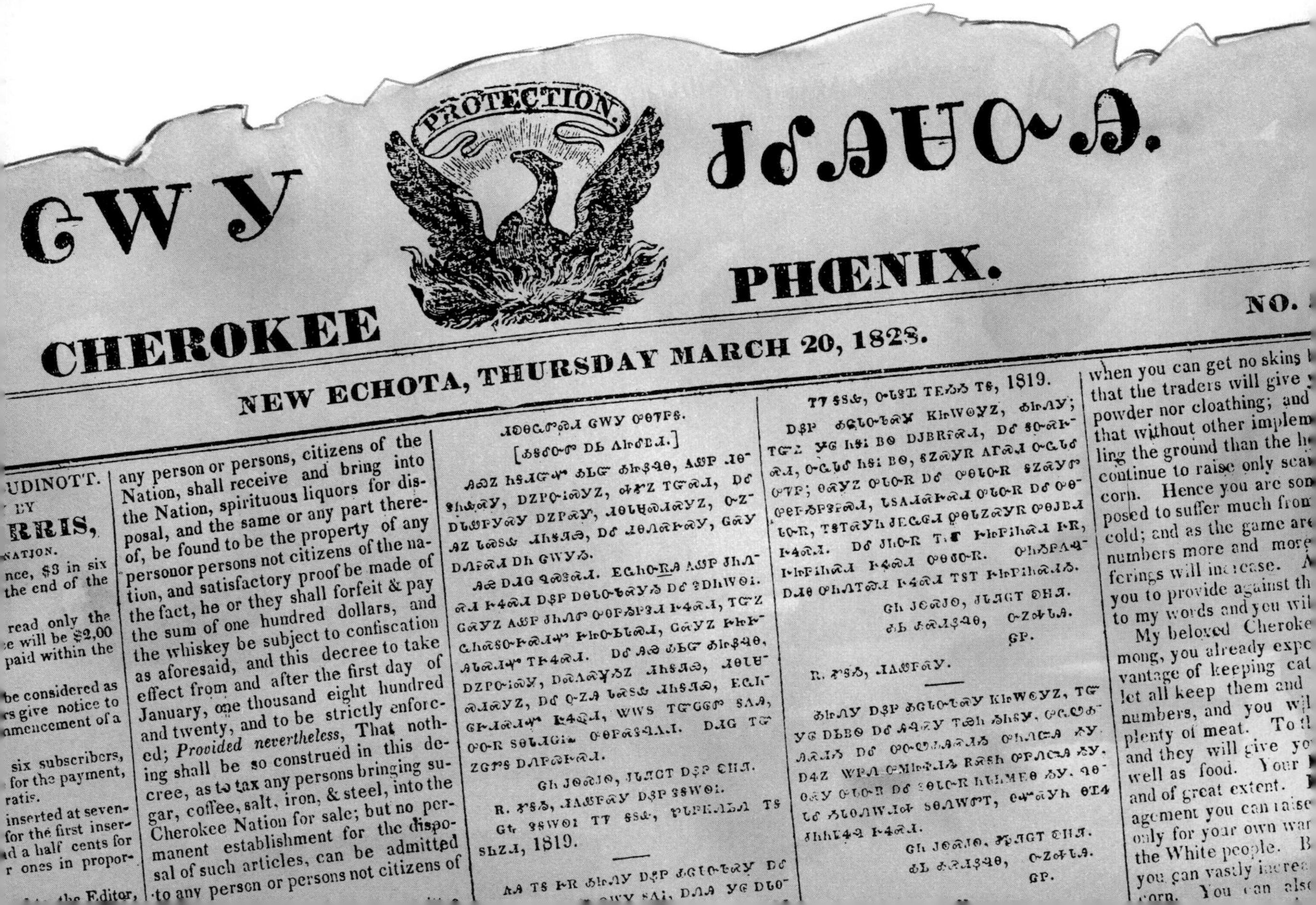

GWY **JᏣᏬᎢᎠ.**

CHEROKEE PROTECTION. **PHŒNIX.**

NO.

NEW ECHOTA, THURSDAY MARCH 20, 1828.

UDINOTT.
RRIS,
NATION.

nce, $3 in six
the end of the

read only the
se will be $2,00
paid within the

be considered as
rs give notice to
mencement of a

six subscribers,
for the payment,
ratis.

inserted at seven-
for the first inser-
ad a half cents for
r ones in propor-

the Editor,

any person or persons, citizens of the Nation, shall receive and bring into the Nation, spirituous liquors for disposal, and the same or any part thereof, be found to be the property of any personor persons not citizens of the nation, and satisfactory proof be made of the fact, he or they shall forfeit & pay the sum of one hundred dollars, and the whiskey be subject to confiscation as aforesaid, and this decree to take effect from and after the first day of January, one thousand eight hundred and twenty, and to be strictly enforced; *Provided nevertheless*, That nothing shall be so construed in this decree, as to tax any persons bringing sugar, coffee, salt, iron, & steel, into the Cherokee Nation for sale; but no permanent establishment for the disposal of such articles, can be admitted to any person or persons not citizens of

ᏙᏯᏍᎠᏯᎠᎦ GWY ᏋᎾᎶᏍ.
[ᎪᏎᏨᏍ ᎠᏞ ᎠᎶᎠᏚᎠ.]

ᎪᏍᏃ ᎲᎦᎩᏨ ᎤᏞᎬ ᏆᏁᏍᏎᏆᎡ, ᎪᏯᏢ .ᎴᏕᎩᎪᎭ, ᏓᏴᏬ-ᎥᎠ�YᏃ, ᎥᏱᏃ ᏔᏠᎯᎢᎡ, ᏕᎣ ᏓᏞᏯᏯᎦᏯ ᏓᏴᏢᎪᏯ, ᎴᎥᎭᎹᎤᎵᎠ�YᏃ, ᎣᏃ ᏆᏃ ᏢᏍᎤᎠ ᏦᏐᎠᏞ, ᏕᎣ ᎴᎴᎠᎳᏢᎤ, ᎦᎦᏯ ᏓᏗᎦᎤᎠ ᏙᎲ GWYᏍᏍ.

ᎪᏍ ᏓᎪᏆ ᏋᏍᏌᏆᎶᎵ. ECHO-ᏓᎶᎠ ᎪᎤᏢ ᏥᎲᎵᎠᎠ ᏆᏍᏯᎠᎠ ᏓᏍᎢᎪ-ᎡᏥᏯᏍ ᏕᎣ ᎢᏓhᎳᎣᎢ. ᎦᎦᏯᏃ ᎪᎤᏢ ᏥᎲᎵᎬ ᏋᏋᏆᏍᏗᎵᎠ ᏆᎦᏆᎡ, ᎢᎦᏃᏃ ᏣᏍᎪᏍᎢᎠᎡᏓᎴᏗ ᎢᎶᏣᏞᎡ, ᎦᎦᏯᏃ ᎢᎢᎢᎠ ᎠᏞᎠᎴᏢ ᎢᏍᏩᏆᎢ. ᏕᎣ ᎪᏍ ᎤᏞᎬ ᏆᏁᏍᏎᏆᎣ. ᏓᏴᏬ-ᎥᎠᏯ, ᏓᏓᎴᏯᏃᏃ ᎴᏍᏌᏆᏍ, ᎴᎴᎢᎵ ᎠᎵᏯᏃᏃ, ᏕᎣ Ꭴ-ᏃᏌ ᏓᏍᏌᏞ ᎴᏍᏌᏆᏍ, ᎡᏟᎵᏕᎴᎢᏆᏯᏘ ᎢᎦᏆᎢᎠ, WᏔᏍ ᏔᏟᏩᏩᏞ ᏍᎠᎠᏃ, ᏋᎣ-ᎡᏍ ᏍᏆᎢᎶᎵᏂ ᏋᏊᏆᏍᎠᎵᏆᎢ. ᏓᎦ ᏔᏟ ᏃᏉᎡᏍ ᏓᏆᏆ-ᏈᎠᎵ.

ᏩᎾ ᏥᏆᏁᏊᏃ, ᏒᎵᎦᏢ ᏓᏍᏴ ᏋᏤᏢᎢ. R. ᎡᏍᏍ, ᏔᎠᏪᏫᏯᏃ ᏓᏍᏴ ᏆᏍᏬᏽᎢ. ᏰᏩ ᏆᏊᏬᏽ ᏔᏘ ᏍᏍᏄᏞ, ᏇᎢᎡᎠᏊ ᎬᏍ ᏍᎭᏃ.ᏂᏆᎵ, 1819.

ᎠᎡ ᏔᏍ ᎡᎡ ᏒᎵᎠᏯᏃ ᏓᏍᏴ ᏋᏤᏢᎢᎠᏓᏯᏍ ᏕᎣ
GWY ᎠᎷᏂ, ᏓᏓᎪ ᏩᏃ ᏍᎠᏊᏬ-

77 ᏍᏍᏚᏍ, ᎣᏃᎵᏳᎡ ᏔᏕᏍᏍ ᏔᏍ, 1819.

ᏓᏍᏴ ᏋᏤᏢᏬ-ᎠᏯᏃ ᎡᏢᏬᏋᏯᏃ, ᏓᏴᎠᏯ; ᏔᏫᏃ ᏰᏤ ᎲᏍᎢ ᏰᎣ ᏓᏥᏨᎢᎠᎵ, ᏕᎣ ᏍᎣ-ᏌᎢᎵ ᏆᏆ, Ꭳ-ᎡᏞᏫ ᎲᏍᎢ ᏰᎣ, ᏍᏎᎠ�YᎡ ᎠᎡᏨᎠ Ꭳ-ᎡᏞᏫ ᎤᏯᏈ; ᎤᎠᏯᏃᏃ ᏋᏬ-ᎡᏍ ᏕᎣ ᏋᏟᎣ-ᎡᏍ ᏍᏎᎠᏯᎠ ᏋᏬᎢᏄᏆᏬᎠᏢ, ᎢᏍᎠᎵᎠᎡᎠᎠ ᏋᏬ-ᎡᏍ ᏕᎣ ᏋᏬᏞᎣ-ᎡᏍ, ᏗᏍᏔᎠᏯᎲ ᏥᎡᏟᎠᏞ ᏋᏬᏟᏎᎠᏯᎡ ᏋᏬᏤᎠ ᏆᏊᏆ. ᏕᎣ ᏥᏟᏬ-ᎡᏍ ᏘᎡ ᎢᎢᏈᎲᏆᎵ ᎡᎡᎡ, ᎢᎢᏈᎲᏆᎵ ᎢᎦᏆᎵ ᏋᏬᏍᏬ-ᎡᏍ. ᏋᎲᏍᏖᏆᎳ ᏆᎦ ᏋᎲᎵᏆᎡᎠ ᎢᎦᏢᎵ ᏔᏍᏘ ᎢᎢᏈᎲᏆᎵᏍ.

ᏲᎲ ᏤᎡᎠᎶ, ᏥᏞᏆᏔ ᎣᎲᎵᎠ. ᏕᎲ ᏋᏆᎵᏌᏆᎶ, Ꭳ-ᏃᏍᏮᏞ.Ꭰ. GP.

R. ᎡᏍᏍ, ᏔᎠᏪᏫᏯᏃ.

ᏓᏴᎠᏯ ᏓᏍᏴ ᏋᏤᏢᏬ-ᎠᏯᏃ, ᏔᏫ ᏰᏤ ᏓᏐᏃ ᏕᎣ ᏍᏍᎯᏯ ᏔᏌᎲ ᏍᎲᏍᏯ. ᎠᎠᏂ ᎠᎡᎵᏍ ᏕᎣ ᏋᏬ-ᎥᎴᎠᏎ ᏋᎲᎵᏍᎠ ᎡᏯ. ᏓᏆᏃ WᎢᎠ ᏨᎲᎢᎠᎵᏎ ᎡᎠᏍᎲ ᏋᏆᎵᏍᏍ ᎡᏯ. Ꭴ ᏋᎠᏯ ᏋᏬ-ᎡᏍ ᏕᎣ ᏍᏬᎵᏋᏬ-ᎡᏍ ᏂᎵᎴᎡᏬ ᎥᏯ. ᎥᏗ Ꮄ ᏍᎶᎠᏯᏨᎶ ᏍᏓᎠᏬᏯ, ᎡᎳᎠᏴᎲ ᎣᏔᏓᏄ ᏕᎲᎴᏍᏯ ᎢᎠᏢᎢ. ᏲᎲ ᏤᎡᎠᎶ, ᏋᏈᎦᏔ ᎣᎲᎵᎠ. ᏕᎲ ᏋᏆᎵᏌᏆᎶ, Ꭳ-ᏃᏍᏮᏞ.Ꭰ. GP.

when you can get no skins
that the traders will give
powder nor cloathing; and
that without other implem
ling the ground than the h
continue to raise only scan
corn. Hence you are son
posed to suffer much from
cold; and as the game are
numbers more and more
ferings will increase. I
you to provide against th
to my words and you wi

My beloved Cherokee
mong, you already expe
vantage of keeping ca
let all keep them and
numbers, and you wi
plenty of meat. To i
and they will give yo
well as food. Your
and of great extent.
agement you can raise
only for your own war
the White people.
you can vastly increa
corn. You can also

A Philadelphia businessman visited with Sequoya and heard the story of the Cherokee's written language. "You have done more for your people," he said, "than if you had given each of them a bag of gold."

Sequoya just smiled his gentle smile. His dream of helping his people, helping them forever, had come true.